Classic Tales

Level 1

CW00508682

The Shoemaker and the Elves

Activity Book and Play

✦ Contents ✦

Name: _____

Class: _____   School: _____

OXFORD
UNIVERSITY PRESS

Before you read, can you match the words with the pictures?

1 dance

2 shoemaker

3 lady

4 elves

5 clothes

6 coins

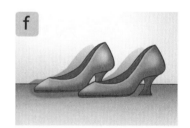

7 shoes

8 family

1 Answer the questions.

1 Is it a woman?
   <u>No, it isn't.</u>

2 Is it a man?
   _____

3 Is it the shoemaker?
   _____

4 Is he old?
   _____

5 Is he in a school?
   _____

6 Is he in his shop? _____

7 Is it a good shop? _____

8 Does it make much money? _____

2 Put the words in the correct order.

1 old the shoemaker It's.
   <u>It's the old shoemaker.</u>

2 shop And his here's.
   _____

3 very isn't a shop It good.
   _____

4 It money doesn't much make.
   _____

→ Pages 4–5

1 Complete the words.

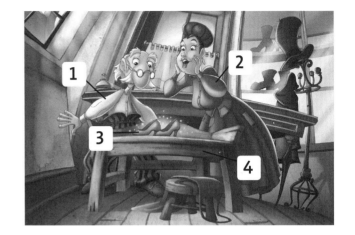

1 It's the s <u>hoemaker</u> .

2 It's his w_____ .

3 It's a p_____ of
    s_____ .

4 It's a t_____ .

2 Choose a, b, or c.

1 The old shoemaker can make one last ...

   a ☐ table   **b** ☐ bag   **c** ☑ pair of shoes

2 His wife says, 'It's ...'

   a ☐ late   **b** ☐ nice   **c** ☐ magic

3 She says, 'Make them in the ...'

   a ☐ morning   **b** ☐ afternoon   **c** ☐ evening

4 In the morning they come ...

   a ☐ in   **b** ☐ down   **c** ☐ up

5 There's something on the ... !

   a ☐ door   **b** ☐ bed   **c** ☐ table

6 It's the ... !

   a ☐ shoes   **b** ☐ trousers   **c** ☐ bags

7 The shoemaker cries, 'Look! ... !'

   a ☐ Money   **b** ☐ Magic   **c** ☐ Breakfast

→ Pages 6–7

1 Write the words.

ldya ___*lady*___   oicsn _____   ethlaer _____

2 Circle the correct words. Then complete the sentences.

1 The ___*shoemaker*___ puts the shoes in the window.

boy (shoemaker) girl

2 A _____ sees them.

lady   girl   man

3 She says, 'What _____ shoes!'

small   magic   beautiful

4 She says, 'I must _____ them.'

take   have   buy

5 She gives the shoemaker three _____ coins.

red   gold   green

6 Now he can make more _____.

bags   hats   shoes

7 He goes out and he buys some more _____.

leather   gold   bread

8 He says, 'Look! Three gold _____!'

shoes   coins   pairs

1 What do they say? Write the words.

I can make two more p_airs_ now.

It's l_____.

Look! More m_____!

2 Find and circle the words. Then complete the sentences.

m	o	r	n	i	n	g	x
d	j	k	q	z	r	t	p
t	v	c	r	i	e	s	b
a	f	b	x	l	g	h	w
b	z	h	v	k	j	p	i
l	a	m	o	r	e	t	f
e	s	e	y	u	r	c	e
v	w	j	c	o	m	e	b

1 The shoemaker says, 'I can make two ___more___ pairs now.'

2 His _____ says, 'It's late.'

3 She says, 'Make them in the _____.'

4 In the morning they _____ down.

5 There's something on the _____!

6 'Look!' _____ the shoemaker.

→ **Pages 10–11**

1 Write the words.

two   some   ~~six~~   three

1 The man has __six__ gold coins.

2 He buys _____ pairs of shoes.

3 Now the shoemaker can make
_____ more pairs of shoes.

4 The shoemaker goes out and he
buys _____ more leather.

2 Put the words in the correct order.

1 the puts in He window shoes the.
He puts the shoes in the window.

2 them A sees man.
_____

3 must I them buy.
_____

4 are gold Here coins six.
_____

5 now can more I make shoes.
_____

6 I money some have.
_____

1 Are the sentences correct? Circle *Yes* or *No*.

1 Now the shoemaker can make two pairs of shoes.   Yes / (No)
2 He makes the shoes in the evening.   Yes / No
3 In the morning he and his wife come down.   Yes / No
4 There's something on the table.   Yes / No
5 They see four pairs of shoes.   Yes / No
6 A family buys the shoes.   Yes / No
7 Now the shoemaker has eight gold coins.   Yes / No

2 Who says what? Write *shoemaker*, *wife*, or *family*.

_____wife_____   _____   _____

1 'I can make three pairs of shoes.'   _____shoemaker_____
2 'We must buy them.'   _____
3 'It's late.'   _____
4 'Look! Magic again.'   _____
5 'What beautiful shoes!'   _____
6 'Make them in the morning.'   _____
7 'Here are nine gold coins.'   _____
8 'Who is making all these shoes?'   _____

→ **Pages 14–15**

Write the words. Then complete the sentences.

a

ehsos ____*shoes*____

b

ihde _____

c

lvese _____

d

pumj _____

e

hactw _____

f

nimdigth _____

1 That night the shoemaker and his wife _____.

2 At _____ they see two little elves!

3 The little elves _____ onto the table.

4 They say, 'Let's make some beautiful ____*shoes*____!'

5 All night the _____ work.

6 The shoemaker and his wife _____.

1 What do they say? Write the words.

1 'We know who h _elps_ us.'
2 'Yes. Two little e_____.'
3 'Let's make some c_____ for them.'
4 'Oh y_____!'

2 Circle the correct words.

1 In the morning the elves **come down** / **run away**.
2 But there's **something** / **some money** on the table.
3 **Four** / **Five** beautiful pairs of shoes!
4 The shoemaker says, '**Now** / **Then** we know.'
5 He says, 'We know who **watches** / **helps** us.'
6 'Yes,' says the shoemaker's **sister** / **wife**.
7 She says, 'But what **can** / **must** we do for them?'
8 The shoemaker says, 'I **see** / **know**.'
9 He says, 'Let's make some **clothes** / **dinner** for them.'

➜ Pages 18–19

1 Answer the questions. Write *Yes* or *No*.

1 Do the shoemaker and
  his wife hide? __Yes.__

2 Do the elves run in at
  midnight? _____

3 Are the elves big? _____

4 Do they like the clothes? _____

5 Do they dance? _____

6 Do they make some shoes? _____

7 Do the elves go? _____

8 Do the elves come back? _____

9 Does the shoemaker make bad shoes now? _____

10 Does the shoemaker work hard? _____

11 Is the shoemaker happy? _____

2 Write the words and number the sentences 1–6.

run   say   leave   ~~comes~~   dance   hide

a ☐ The elves put on the new clothes and they _____.

b ☐ Then the shoemaker and his wife _____.

c ☐ Then the elves _____, 'Goodbye, Shoemaker!'

d ☐1 Night __comes__ .

e ☐ At midnight the little elves _____ in.

f ☐ The shoemaker and his wife _____ the clothes
  on the table.

Play

Act the play.

Characters

 Chorus   Shoemaker

 Wife   Lady

 Man 1
(no words to speak)   Man 2

 Father   Mother

 Girl   Elves

→ Pages 2–3   **Scene 1**

Chorus: Who's this? It's the shoemaker. And here's his shop. It isn't a very good shop. It doesn't make much money.

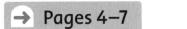 **→ Pages 4–7**

Scene 2

Shoemaker: One last pair of shoes. That's all I can make.

Wife: It's late. Make them in the morning.

Scene 3

Chorus: In the morning they come down. There's something on the table! It's the shoes!

Shoemaker: Look! Magic!

Chorus: He puts the shoes in the window.

Lady: What beautiful shoes! I must buy them. Here are three gold coins.

Scene 4

Chorus: The shoemaker goes out and he buys some more leather.

Shoemaker *(to Man 1)*: I have some money. Look! Three gold coins!

→ Pages 8–12 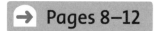  ### *Scene 5*

Shoemaker: I can make two more pairs now.
Wife: It's late. Make them in the morning.

Scene 6

Chorus: In the morning they come down. There's something on the table! Two pairs of shoes.

Shoemaker: Look! More magic!

Chorus: He puts the shoes in the window.

Man 2: What beautiful shoes! I must buy them. Here are six gold coins.

Scene 7

Chorus: The shoemaker buys some more leather.

Shoemaker: I can make three pairs of shoes.
Wife: It's late. Make them in the morning.

 *Scene 8*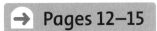

Chorus: In the morning they come down. There's something on the table! Three pairs of shoes.

Shoemaker: Look! Magic again.

 *Scene 9*

Girl: What beautiful shoes!
Mother: We must buy them.
Father: Here are nine gold coins.
Shoemaker: Who is making all these shoes?

Scene 10

Chorus: That night the shoemaker and his wife hide. At midnight they see two little elves.

Elves: Here's the leather! Let's work!

Chorus: All night they work. The shoemaker and his wife watch.

→ Pages 16–19

 *Scene 11*

Chorus: In the morning the elves run away.

Shoemaker: Now we know who helps us.
Wife: Yes. But what can we do for them?
Shoemaker: I know. Let's make some clothes
for them.

Scene 12

Chorus: At midnight the elves run in.

Elves: What's this? It's something for us!

Chorus: They put on the new clothes.

Elves: Now it's time for us to go. Goodbye!

Scene 13

Chorus: The elves never come back. But
the shoemaker works hard. And he
is happy.

 *The End*